MAKING FIRST
DOWNS IN LIFE

MAKING FIRST DOWNS IN LIFE

A Student Athlete's Guide For Success
On And Off The Field

MAURICE DOWELL

Making First Downs in Life

First Published by MO Publishing in 2020

Copyright © Maurice Dowell

ISBN: 978-1-64660-000-7

Printed in the USA

MO Publishing

MO Publishing

DEDICATION

If you want to be Division 1, then this is the book for you. If you want to make A's and B's, then this is the book for you. If you want to be a starter on your school's varsity team, then this is the book for you. If you want to qualify for academic scholarships, then this book is the book for you. If you want to make the playoffs and win state, this is the book for you. This book holds the key that will help you reach the first downs and wins in life. In each chapter, you will find positive affirmations, self-talk, action steps, and quotes. These tools are there to help you be interactive with the text. After each positive affirmation, you will also find a football story of mine relating to the chapter. I encourage you as a reader to take notes and to stay on a chapter for as long as you need. Do not move on to the next chapter until you have completed the action steps for the chapter you are on.

TABLE OF CONTENTS

FORWARD

*M*aking First Downs in Life is a book/workbook that will guide, inspire, and challenge you as well as make you strive to do better. It's a great resource for pastors who are cutting-edge and are really concerned and care about helping parents and student athletes in their congregation. The book can help pastors to better help parents to become more informed about how they can help their children position themselves for great opportunities. From my years of knowing and observing Maurice, I have watched him succeed as a student athlete on and off the field. I noticed how he worked hard to position himself to better himself whether on the field or off the field. And in *Making First Downs in Life*, Maurice does a marvelous job of sharing the same life skill principles that helped him to help student athletes as they endeavor to become better as a student and athlete in a very competitive society. The author is transparent as he shares a piece of his story in each chapter. This book will help that student-athlete become a better person mentally, financially, and spiritually. It is my prayer and belief that after you—the pastor, the teacher, the coach, the counselor, and the parent—have read this book and have encouraged student-athletes to do the same as well as engage in the action steps after each chapter, you will see great results.

Dr. Clinton P. Cornelius

Senior Pastor

Peaceful Believers Church

Fort Meade, Florida

INTRODUCTION

The principles throughout this book are what allowed me to have football and academic scholarships to choose from. I am currently a college student who is going to school on a full-ride scholarship. I am a Regents Honor Scholar at Langston University in Langston, Oklahoma. I also received a football scholarship to play at Langston and would never have known about Langston University or the McCabe Honors program without the football skills with which God blessed me. Consequently, I made the decision to not play football and chose to focus on my academics. As a student-athlete, you don't have to choose that route, but you always want to give yourself options.

From elementary to high school, I was part of the gifted and talented program. I took honors classes when they were offered and took a college level course in my senior year of high school. My high school GPA was a 3.9; I only had one B from my freshman to senior year. In football, I started on the varsity team since my sophomore year. I was first team all-district running back, second team all-district defensive back, and Safety of the Year in my senior year. I also qualified for state in track throughout my high school years. I am currently a supplemental instructor for biology and a tutor in the writing center at Langston University. I made President's Honor Roll in my freshman year and Dean's Honor Roll in my sophomore year of college. In my freshman year of college, I held the title of Mr. Regents, and I now hold the title of Mr. Scholars Club.

I decided to write this book to help others reach their dreams. I live by the principles in this book, and they have helped me reach important milestones in my life. The journey is not over yet, and I am still striving every day. I understand that if I am not growing, I am dead. From books like *The Alchemist*, I learned I am who I choose to be. I know that at the end of the day, I make the choice of what it is going to be, who I am going to be, and how I am going to do it.

For as long as I can remember, I planned to go to college and wanted to play football in college. But the opportunity did not just come to me. It was planned. I knew I wanted a football scholarship, and I knew I wanted an academic scholarship. To give yourself the best chance in life, you cannot put all of your eggs in one basket. One day after high school, college, or the pros, you will need to continue to get first downs in something else. The principles throughout this book will also help you pursue whatever the future holds for you. This book will teach you to be balanced and to keep making first downs in life.

How to utilize this book and get the most out of it.

- Answer and complete action steps.

- Discuss huddle up questions and answers with your team in group discussions.

- Stay on each chapter for as long as you need.

- Read self-talks aloud and multiple times throughout the week.

- Highlight quotes that stand out to you, refer to them throughout the week for inspiration.

CHAPTER 1
GAME PLAN

Positive Affirmation - I am thankful. I am strong. I am blessed. I will achieve success!

It was the year 2015, on a Sunday in the great state of Oklahoma. I was in my junior year of the football season. On this blessed Sunday, I was at the field house getting my game plan to prepare for the team I was going to face. This game plan was different because it was the first time my high school football team had been to the playoffs in a long time. Honestly, I can say I did not take the game plan as seriously as I needed to take it. I always felt it was unnecessary to plan the offense and defense we would run against the opposing team. I just wanted to play the game and have fun. I was immature mentally when it came to planning for opposing opponents. But I have won in many aspects of my life because I took planning seriously. I planned throughout my whole childhood to be ready for the opportunity to play football at the next level as well as being able to go to college to pursue a degree. From elementary school to high school, I always planned before the school year started that I would earn straight A's.

In life, you should have a vision that symbolizes your dreams and values. A game plan will help you to stay on track, reach your dreams, and follow your values. A game plan can be defined as a carefully thought-out strategy or course of action as in politics, business, or personal affairs. You must have a well-thought-out game plan before reaching first downs in life. Most people are not happy with where they are in life. Most people do not thoroughly map out where they want to be in life. Most people attack life day by day with no plan. On the contrary, people who are successful have a game plan. I am reminded of the ant and the grasshopper fable where you really need a plan to succeed. In "The Ant and the Grasshopper," the ants planned and worked hard during the summer, spring, and fall gathering food to prepare for winter. The grasshopper did not plan but instead ate and played all summer, spring, and fall. But when winter came, the grasshopper was cold, miserable, and hungry. At the end of the story, the grasshopper learns a valuable lesson about the importance of preparing for the future.

Do not be the grasshopper. Plan to be successful in the summer, spring, fall, and winter. I did not get a football scholarship by just going to practice. It started all the way back when I was catching footballs in my backyard with my dad when I was five years old. It was the time that I spent two to three times a week outside of actual football practice doing football workouts with my older brother. I remember vividly training at The Next Level Sports with coach Aso Pogi. As a high school coach, Pogi was very influential in that he molded me to not just be a successful athlete but also a successful young man. I also remember Pogi having me plan, at the beginning of my football season, for how many yards I would get, catches I would receive, and touchdowns I would score. He trained me since eighth grade and was a football coach at my high school from my sophomore through senior year. He was an outstanding coach, and he always pushed me and my team to be our very best. I will forever be grateful for what he has poured into me and the positive impact he has made in my life.

Likewise, I did not get an academic scholarship by just going to school. It also started all the way from when I was doing math flashcards with my brothers growing up. It was the time that I planned to go to SAT and ACT preps. It takes planning to be the very best student-athlete you can possibly be. Your guidance counselors at your school are wonderful people who you can reach out to make sure you are on track. My high school guidance counselor, Tammy Fritz, was phenomenal in helping me get signed up for ACTs and making sure I was eligible to receive scholarships and play college sports. I was blessed to have such a dedicated high school counselor. It all requires you planning to reach out to your high school guidance counselors. If you can plan to hang out with your friends, then you can plan your future to ensure your success.

How To Make A Game Plan That Will Get First Downs

1. Ask yourself, what exactly is it that I want? In order to have a goal, you first need a vision. You must ask yourself what exactly it is that you want. This is where you close your eyes and imagine the type of house you want to live in, the job you want to have, and the car you expect to drive. You should not set limits on how big you dream.

_____

_____

_____

_____

_____

_____

2. Write down what you want. According to a study done by Gail Matthews at Dominican University, those who wrote down their goals accomplished significantly more than those who did not write down their goals. With your vision, create a list of goals and plan how you will get there. In your vision, you might want to become a doctor. Create small step-by-step goals that will help you reach that dream of becoming a doctor. The more precise and detailed you are, the better.

_____

_____

_____

_____

_____

_____

_____

3. **Set a time frame in which the goal needs be accomplished**. Some of the goals you might have are small goals. A small goal is something that can be achieved in a short period of time. Set time frames or benchmarks for when you want to accomplish that goal. This will help you to stay on track and continue to move towards reaching the vision you have for your life. Remember, many of your goals are reached through small achievements. You cannot graduate from high school or college without passing that first year. Your small achievement would be passing the first year.

_____

_____

_____

_____

_____

_____

_____

4. Organize it into a sequence of step-by-step actions you need to take. Now that you have your goals and time frames, you need to organize them. Write them out in a way that you can follow. This is the game plan that will help you reach first downs in your life and continue to get you closer to achieving your dreams.

_____

_____

_____

_____

_____

_____

_____

QUOTES

- "The first step is you have to say that you can."- **Will Smith**

- "Before you can get what you want, you have to know what you want and make a game plan to get it." -**Jefferey Gitomer**

- "Get past all the emotions that come along with the experience and get to the important stuff. Recognize what it is that you want, put a game plan together and take those steps to making a quality choice." -**Bill Kidney**

- "In every aspect of life, have a game plan and then do your best to achieve it." -**Alan Kulwicki**

- "You were born to win. But to be a winner, you must plan to win, prepare to win and expect to win." -**Zig Ziglar**

Self-Talk - Staying focused is what separates the mediocre from the great. Whatever I start, I must finish. Quitting is the easy way out, and nothing in life comes easy. Life is a blessing, and life is a gift. I am not just going to talk about what I want to do anymore, but I am going to plan and do whatever it takes to make my plans a reality.

PERSONAL ACTION STEPS

1.) Write where you want to be in life two years from now.

_____

_____

_____

_____

_____

_____

_____

2.) Write three goals for your academic school year, three goals for your athletic season, and three other goals you may have.

ACADEMIC-

_____

_____

_____

_____

_____

_____

_____

ATHLETIC-

_____
_____
_____
_____
_____
_____
_____

OTHER-

_____
_____
_____
_____
_____
_____
_____

3.) What grades do you plan to receive in the classroom over the next two years?

_____
_____
_____
_____
_____
_____
_____

TEAM ACTION STEP

1.) Find an accountability partner on your team. What is one of his goals for the team's season? *If they do not have any, help them create some goals to be successful.*

_____

_____

_____

_____

_____

_____

_____

2.) Talk to your head coach and your position coach to find out team goals for the year.

_____

_____

_____

_____

_____

_____

_____

3.) Make an appointment with your guidance counselor to make sure you are eligible to play at the college level. *NCAA Clearinghouse and NAIA eligibility*

_____

_____

_____

_____

_____

_____

_____

HUDDLE UP AND DISCUSS

1.) Why is it important to have a personal game plan and goals?

_____

_____

_____

_____

_____

_____

2.) Why is it important to have team goals?

_____

_____

_____

_____

_____

_____

3.) Why do you feel that players may struggle with buying into team goals?

_____

_____

_____

_____

_____

_____

_____

CHAPTER 2
FILM WORK/STUDY

* Positive Affirmation - I have discipline. I am dedicated to being successful. I choose to be happy today. No obstacle will be able to stop me in my life.

My head high school football coach, John Herbert, and his coaching staff went out of their way every week to print out game plans for the upcoming games. On the game plan, you could find the opposing team's roster and see who started at each position. I remember often after long practices, they would be in the main office, watching film and studying tendencies, so they could express those to the team and share them in the game plan. For the playoff game, it was not any different. There was an abundance of information to help my team be ready to compete for our first playoff win. From offense of schemes, special teams, and defense of schemes, it had it all. Unfortunately, some of the players left the plans in their cars the whole week and never touched them after Sunday's meeting. I know because of Coach Herbert and his staff's detailed studying and planning, they were able to go on and win a state championship title at their next coaching assignment. I also now know that it is up to the players to take the game plan seriously and study it to be able to win. In my life, I have studied many of my personal game plans and was successful because of it. I can vividly remember watching film with my former high school football teammate, Kaieem Caesar. He now plays college football at The Ohio University, a Division 1 school. I also watched videos on ACT prep and what it took to get a degree in nursing. I did this because I knew one day, football was going to come to an end and I wanted to have options outside of football. Giving myself options allowed me the opportunity to receive a football scholarship from a historical black college as well as a full-ride academic scholarship. Whatever other option in life you may choose, you must dedicate yourself to studying both your sport and that option.

When I was younger, my father enrolled me and two of my brothers in piano lessons. I wanted to play the piano like the greats, so I practiced every day until I did not mess up. My brothers, on the other hand, would not practice until the day we actually had piano lessons. This caused them to stay where they were and not progress as quickly I did. I excelled at piano, and to this day, I can still play the piano well. On the other hand, my two brothers cannot play the piano. Just because they were in piano lessons does not mean they will be able to play piano. They did not study and practice. Therefore, they did not reap success. It is one thing to be part of a team and be in a classroom and have goals. But if you do not practice and study, you will not reap success.

In order to succeed, you have to study your game plan. In life, you must be dedicated to learning about what it takes to reach your goals. You are not going to wake up one day and magically be where you want to be in life. Successful people are focused people. You must control the controllable. Do not waste your time on meaningless distractions. You must be disciplined enough to make your goals a priority. We all have 24 hours in a day, and those 24 hours determine our future success. You must learn how to suffer now so you can enjoy later. In Aesop's fable, "The Crow and the Pitcher," the crow was half dead of thirst and came across a pitcher that had once been full of water. The crow put his beak in the pitcher and realized there was very little water left in the pitcher, so he could not reach the water. He tried and tried but ultimately had to give up in despair. Then a thought came to him; he took a pebble and dropped it into the pitcher. Then he took another pebble and dropped it into the pitcher, and on and on he went. Soon, the water rose high enough so that he could drink the water and finally quench his thirst. This crow was dedicated to quenching his thirst, and if he did not know that the pebbles would cause the water to rise, he would have died of dehydration. It is important for you to think and come up with every possible way for you to reach your goals so that you don't give up on them. This is why it's important to study your game plan.

Be like the crow.

Here are some pebbles you can put in the classroom pitcher.

1. Mute or turn off your phone so you can be fully engaged. You are in school to learn. Twitter, Snapchat, and Instagram can wait. Be fully engaged in what the teacher is teaching. You are in school to learn, not hang out.

2. Respect your teacher as well as your peers. Be respectful. If you want respect, you have to learn how to give it. Be polite and have manners. Speak in a way that is professional.

3. Get good grades. Do not be afraid to ask for help. Your teachers are there because they want you to succeed. It takes effort to earn good grades, so it is not just going to be handed to you. Turn in every assignment on time and always put forth your best work. If you want to play sports at the next level, your grades must be good.

-Here are some pebbles you can put in your sport pitcher.

1. Always be on time to practice. If practice starts at 1 p.m. Be there at 12:30 p.m. Get there 30 minutes early to get warmed up and ready for practice. Be the first there and the last to leave if possible.

2. Leave drama/attitude at the door. Do not let your emotions get in the way of a good practice. Drop the girlfriend and boyfriend problems. If you have drama with a teammate, settle it and do not let it get in the way of the team's success.

3. Stay competitive. Practice like it is gameday. Do not just go through the motions. If you are on the scout team or junior varsity, take mental reps. You may not be a starter, but you never know when they will call you in so you want to be ready. Always compete to work the hardest on the field or court.

HOW TO STUDY YOUR GAME PLAN

-Set aside one day out of the week where you intentionally look over your game plan. You must always know what your goals are. Many people create goals, and in about a week, they forget what their goals were.

- Do an internet search for what it takes to reach your goals. If you want to become a doctor, lawyer, NBA or NFL sports star, physical therapist, school teacher, or whatever it is, study what classes you are required to take in college. Does it require a degree? Are there programs you can get into to ensure your future success?

- You must desire to find a way. There is **NO** cheat code or secret hack to becoming successful. Do not waste your time trying to find ways to become rich quick.

QUOTES-

- "Success is no accident. It is hard work, perseverance, learning, studying, sacrifice, and most of all, love of what you are doing or learning to do." -**Pele**

- "Prepare for the unknown by studying how others in the past have coped with the unforeseeable and the unpredictable." -**George S. Patton**

- "The person you will be in five years is based on the books you read and the people you surround yourself with today." -**Unknown**

- "The will to succeed is important, but what's more important is the will to prepare." -**Bobby Knight**

"With the new day comes new strength and new thoughts." -**Eleanor Roosevelt**

Self-Talk - Dedication is what separates the winners from the losers. I must have discipline in all areas of my life. I have to value myself enough to always do the best that I can do and be the best that I can be. I will put my all into it, or I will not do it all. No one will spoon feed me everything in life. I have to set out on my own and find out what it takes to get to where I want to be in life. I don't know what I don't know, but I only know from searching and studying, putting in that time and trying to know everything it takes to get first downs in life.

PERSONAL ACTION STEPS

1.) **Set your goal or game plan as your background on your cell phone. In today's society, most people have a cell phone. When you are on your phone, read over that goal or game plan.**

_____

_____

_____

_____

_____

_____

_____

2.) **What pebble for the classroom will you focus on for this week?**

_____

_____

_____

_____

_____

_____

_____

3.) What days will you study? Specific days and specific times. *Ex. On Monday from 6 p.m. - 6:30 p.m., I will study for bio, and from 6:30 p.m. – 7 p.m., I will watch film for my sport.*

_____

_____

_____

_____

_____

_____

_____

TEAM ACTION STEPS

1.) With a teammate that plays the same position, go over plays and study together.

_____

_____

_____

_____

_____

_____

_____

2.) Talk to your coach and ask him what you can do to improve as an athlete. Study how to get better. Write how you will improve.

_____

_____

_____

_____

_____

_____

_____

HUDDLE UP AND DISCUSS

1. Why is it important to study and to take film seriously?

_____

_____

_____

_____

_____

_____

_____

2. What can the coach do better to help you prepare for your games?

_____

_____

_____

_____

_____

_____

_____

3. What can players do better to prepare for practices and be ready for the games?

_____

_____

_____

_____

_____

_____

_____

CHAPTER 3
GAME DAY

* Positive Affirmation – I do not fear the fire... I am the fire. I was not made to give up. The only person who can defeat me is myself. I believe in the person I dream of becoming.

November 13, 2015, it was game day. Ulrich Stadium was packed, and the city of Cache was excited to see the football team win its first playoff game in many years. I felt as if I had electricity running through my body. My team was hyped, and we were ready to win this game and proceed to the next round. On the first play of the game, I missed a tackle, and the running back ran for about 60 yards. He was tackled short of the touchdown. I did not let that affect me, and I continued to play every snap to my best ability. I understood I could not let that one error affect how I would finish the game. As a student-athlete, you cannot let mistakes define you. Many times in my life, I have fallen short or failed, but I always got up. I continued to try, pressed forward, and never gave up. I used to struggle with writing, but I continued to working on my skills to become a better writer. I was not the strongest in the weight room growing up, but that never stopped me from working out to my best ability. Taking it day by day and learning from my mistakes allowed me to accomplish more than I could have ever imagined.

After the tedious work of making a game plan and studying, you are now ready to attack your goals. You are prepared to head to kick off, knowing what it takes to accomplish your goals. With that being said, it is still you against the world. Life will not hand you what you want because you made a plan and studied it. Life will hit you with the unexpected, but you must be ready to play. You must remember it is the first downs that lead to touchdowns. Stay true to your game plan no matter what life hits you with. Slow and steady will win the race. In Aesop's fable, "The Tortoise and the Hare," the hare boasted about being fast and how no other animal could beat him in a race. He challenged the animals, and a tortoise accepted his challenge. The hare laughed sarcastically thinking it was a joke, but the tortoise was serious. So, soon after the race started, the hare ran ahead, laughing and making fun of the tortoise; he laid down and took a nap. But the tortoise kept slowly going and going. He passed by the hare quietly and continued to head closer to the finish line. When the hare woke up, to his surprise, he saw the tortoise crossing the finishing line and winning the race. This story shows that slow and steady does indeed win the race. It also shows you should not worry about how fast other people are moving in life because you never know what obstacles they may face along the way. Taking it yard by yard and inch by inch to get first downs in the game is key.

How to take it yard by yard and slow and steady - Hastily jumping into an activity can cause problems. A more consistent and orderly approach can be ideal and give you better results even if it is a slower approach. For example, if you want to become faster, going to the gym and running as fast as you can for as long as you can will not do much to make you faster. Taking it slow, working technique, working flexibility, and working leg strength over time will get you better results. It is the same concept for the classroom. If you want to pass a test, cramming all the information in one night would be less effective than studying consistently over a period time.

One way to take it slow and steady is not to make excuses. I know that life sometimes can deal out bad cards. As someone who wants to be successful, you must accept the things that are out of your control. The pain you may be experiencing could be your mom's, dad's, friend's, teacher's, or coach's fault, but it is your own responsibility to deal with it and fix it. An example of someone who did not make excuses is former NFL linebacker, Ray Lewis. He is a two-time Defensive Player of the Year and a Super Bowl MVP. He played his entire 17-year career with the Baltimore Ravens. Lewis was born in Florida and had a childhood that was not always stable. Ray Lewis once said, "What I went through as a child, a child shouldn't go through. I became bitter, I became very bitter and I became pissed off young." Lewis' mother had him when she was only 16, and his father was largely absent in his life. He was the oldest of four siblings and became the man of the house. He helped his sisters with their hair and made sure his younger brother got to daycare on time. Even with all those responsibilities, Lewis made all state in football and all state in wrestling in high school, breaking previous records that his father had set. Lewis is a great example of how to channel your **pain** into something **productive.** He never made excuses, and he utilized the cards that life had dealt to him.

QUOTES-

- "Some people want it to happen, some wish it would happen, others make it happen." -**Michael Jordan**

- "All our dreams can come true if we have the courage to pursue them." -**Walt Disney**

- "The most difficult thing is the decision to act, the rest is merely tenacity. The fears are paper tigers. You can do anything you decide to do. You can act to change and control your life; and the procedure, the process is its own reward." -**Amelia Earhart**

- "The will to win, the desire to succeed, the urge to reach your full potential... these are the keys that will unlock the door to personal excellence." -**Confucius**

- "Never, never, never give up." -**Winston Churchill**

* **Self-Talk** -I will win the day. I will keep the ball rolling in my life. I will continue to push through what life throws at me. I am committed to moving step by step to reach my goals. I understand that first downs will lead to a touchdown. I understand that slow and steady will win the race. I understand that I do not have to worry about how fast the person next to me is moving in life. I refuse to doubt myself. Every day I will win the day.

PERSONAL ACTION STEPS

1.) Keep taking it play by play and day by day. Make a commitment to do better in at least one area of your life even if it is as little as making your bed every day when you get up in the morning.

_____

_____

_____

_____

_____

_____

_____

2.) Next time you fall, get back up and continue the race. It does not matter how slow you get up, just get up.

_____

_____

_____

_____

_____

_____

TEAM ACTION STEP

1.) Encourage your teammates to keep on going. Whether it's in the weight room, football field, basketball court, soccer field, track, etc.

_____

_____

_____

_____

_____

_____

_____

HUDDLE UP AND DISCUSS

1.) Why is it important to keep going even after you make a mistake?

_____

_____

_____

_____

_____

_____

_____

2.) What are some ways that the team can encourage each other on and off the field?

_____

_____

_____

_____

_____

_____

_____

3.) What are some ways you can move forward, as a team, after a bad practice?

_____

_____

_____

_____

_____

_____

_____

CHAPTER 4
OFFENSE AND DEFENSE

* **Positive Affirmation** - I am capable of all things that I set my mind to do. I am enough. I believe that I am more than a conqueror.

The score at halftime was 10 to 10. Our offense battled against the opposing defense the entire night. There was not one moment when I gave up on my team. Our offense took it play by play to try to get first downs. We motivated each other and held each other accountable. We never underestimated ourselves and offered our very best. Having my team with me was one of the best feelings. We all offered individual talents, and together they could not be stopped.

In football, you have four snaps to get a first down and move the ball forward over a distance of 10 yards. You have a defense that is facing you, trying to stop you from getting where you need to be. The defense represents the people in your life who doubt you. These are the people in your life who do not want you to succeed and want you to fall short of your goals. On the offensive side, you have people on your team trying to reach a common goal. These are the people in life that help and motivate you. They have the common goal of keeping the chains moving, so they will do whatever it takes to make that happen. You need to surround yourself with people who will elevate you. Remove yourself from any negative relationships that may stop you from reaching your goals. It's also key to never underestimate yourself. In Aesop's fable, "The Hart and the Hunter," the hart was drinking at a river. He was looking at his reflection, just admiring and boasting about his beautiful antlers. He then noticed how small and weak his legs were and was feeling down about them. Then out of nowhere, a hunter walked up and shot an arrow. Hart dashed off and realized that thanks to his legs, he survived. At this point in the story, it teaches us not to underestimate ourselves, and that our so-called weakness can be our strength. Now when the hart was looking at his legs, his antlers got stuck in the trees. The hunter caught up to the hart and killed it. This part of the fable shows us that we need to be humble because it can be our positive strengths that get us caught up and killed. You can get first downs in life if you remain humble and do not underestimate yourself.

TIPS TO BE NOT UNDERESTIMATE YOURSELF

1. Make a list of your strengths and positive traits. Doing this will keep you from focusing on your weaknesses all the time. It is a 100 percent necessary that you feel good about yourself but do not become arrogant. A good way you can add to the list is to ask your friends, teammates, teachers, or family to tell you your strengths.

2. Try not to compare yourself to others all the time. In today's society, social media has glorified fictional lifestyles. It is easy to find yourself comparing yourself to these social media influencers. You should not do this because they usually only shine light on what is good in their lives and not the negative things.

QUOTES-

- "It's not whether you get knocked down. It's whether you get up." -**Vince Lombardi**

- "Believe in yourself, take on your challenges, dig deep within yourself to conquer fears. Never let anyone bring you down. You got to keep going." -**Chantal Sutherland**

- "It always seems impossible until it is done." -**Nelson Mandela**

- "You have to be able to accept failure to get better." -**LeBron James**

- "It is during our darkest moments that we must focus to see the light." -**Aristotle**

* **Self-Talk** - When life gives me lemons, I will make lemonade. There is nothing that will stop me from achieving my goals. I choose to surround myself with people who push me to do better. I will look at myself in the mirror every day and know that I am enough. I will no longer doubt myself or underestimate myself.

PERSONAL ACTION STEP

1.) Do something you have always wanted to do but thought you could not do because you underestimated yourself. Run a mile, do 50 pushups, start a YouTube channel, or write a book.

_____

_____

_____

_____

_____

_____

_____

TEAM ACTION STEP

1.) Be humble. Respect your opponent's strengths and their weaknesses. Do not get beat because you think it is going to be an easy win. Write down your opponent's strengths and weaknesses.

_____

_____

_____

_____

_____

_____

_____

HUDDLE UP AND DISCUSS

1.) Why is it important to go into each game like it is the hardest game of the season?

_____

_____

_____

_____

_____

_____

_____

2.) What are three qualities of a successful team?

_____

_____

_____

_____

_____

_____

_____

3.) What do you offer to the team as an individual?

_____

_____

_____

_____

_____

_____

_____

CHAPTER 5
SPECIAL TEAMS

* **Positive Affirmation** I will learn from my mistakes. I will grow and be better than I was yesterday. My mistakes are life lessons, not life sentences.

In football, there is a group of individuals considered special teams. They come in the game when it is a kickoff, field goal, or punt. Most people forget about special teams because they rarely get on the field. In my opinion, special team members are the most important individuals on a team. Many teams in football risk turning the ball over instead of putting their special teams out on the field. In life, you must know when to put your special teams on the field. Sometimes you will fall short, but that is okay. You see a punter comes in on a fourth down to kick the ball to the other team. In doing this, he is putting his team in a better position to potentially score a touchdown. Kicking the ball away also gives the offense time to regroup and see how they will attack the defense in the next series. Special teams in your life can be someone coming into your life as a relief. This relief comes in the form of a mentor, parent, friend, or spiritual being. You need someone to help you out when you do not achieve a first down. You will fall short in life but do not let it define you. Bring in your special teams and take your time to assess the situation and how you will attack the defense to get that first down. While special teams are on the field, learn what you can do better so the next time you are out on the field, you do not make the same mistakes. In Aesop's fable, "The Lion, the Donkey, and the Fox," a lion, donkey, and fox were hunting together. They caught a lot of food and decided to split it with each other. The lion asked the donkey to divide the food. The donkey divided the food into equal portions. This made the lion extremely angry, so he killed the donkey. The lion then turned around and asked the fox to divide the food. The fox wasted no time and gave the lion a large portion of the food and gave himself a little portion. The lion then asked the fox who taught you to divide so fairly. The fox then replied that he learned from the donkey. In this fable, the fox learned what he should do while it was not his turn. He learned from the mistakes of another. When special teams are in, you should be learning what you can do better to get first downs. Do not take this time as a time to sit around and do nothing.

TIPS TO BE LIKE THE FOX - Patiently wait your turn but while waiting, learn as much as you can from the person ahead of you. If it is in the classroom and you have a speech or presentation to do, watch and listen to the person who goes before you. Write down the mistakes they make and be sure you do not make those mistakes. Also, take note of what they do well so you can be sure you do those things well. If it is in the sport you play, take note of the person who starts the game. Learn from them. Analyze what they do wrong and the mistakes they make, so you do not make those same mistakes. If you watch and learn in the classroom and in your sport, you will put yourself in a better position to be successful.

QUOTES-

- "Making mistakes is a lot better than not doing anything." **-Billie Joe Armstrong**

- "The key is to keep company only with people who uplift you, whose presence calls forth your best." **-Epictetus**

- "Set your goals high, and don't stop till you get there."- **Bo Jackson**

- "A true champion will fight through anything." **-Floyd Mayweather, Jr.**

- "Go for it now. The future is promised to no one." - **Wayne Dyer**

Self-Talk There is always room to grow. I will learn from my mistakes. I will enjoy the process of reaching my dreams. I will keep on trying again even if I don't get a first down in life the first time around. I am wise enough to say that I may need help/relief from special teams. I will not take time off from my goals. If I am not actively going for my goal or studying what it takes, I will not obtain that goal.

Action Steps Find someone who can hold you accountable for reaching your goals and following your game plan. This person will be a part of your special teams. If you need relief, let them know. If you need advice, let them know. If you feel like you cannot go on, let them know.

PERSONAL ACTION STEPS

1.) When it is not your turn, wait patiently and learn from others ahead of you.

_____

_____

_____

_____

_____

_____

_____

2.) Write down two people you can call or reach out to if you need help and/or advice. These can be mentors, teachers, coaches, pastors, etc.

_____

_____

_____

_____

_____

_____

TEAM ACTION STEPS

1.) Plan to have bonding time with your team and just chill.

_____

_____

_____

_____

2.) Write something you have learned throughout the season thus far.

_____

_____

_____

_____

HUDDLE UP AND DISCUSS

1.) What is the importance of taking mental reps and watching the person ahead of you?

_____

_____

_____

_____

_____

_____

_____

2.) How do you recharge?

_____

_____

_____

_____

_____

_____

_____

3.) What impact do you have on others as an individual?

_____

_____

_____

_____

_____

_____

_____

How to identify first downs in your life.

A first down is any accomplishment that is leading to your big success. Below is a list of examples of first downs and their touchdowns associated with them:

- Finishing your homework is a first down. Acing the test would be a touchdown.

- Going up 10 pounds on your bench press max is a first down.

- Going up 2 points on your ACT is a first down. Achieving necessary score to get into college would be a touchdown.

- Getting your permit is a first down and then getting your driver's license would be a touchdown.

- Getting to play special teams as a freshman is a first down.

– Passing a math test is a first down, and passing that class would be a touchdown.

– Getting a job interview would be a first down, and getting the job would be a touchdown.

– Getting accepted into a college would be a first down, and getting academic scholarships or sports scholarships would be a touchdown.

ABOUT THE AUTHOR
MAURICE R. DOWELL

Born in raised in Oklahoma, Maurice Dowell is an entrepreneur currently pursuing a degree in nursing at Langston University. He founded MO Publishing Company and is a social media influencer. He is an honors scholar and supplemental instructor at Langston University. He is on the President's Honor Roll as well as the Dean's Honor Roll. He was elected as Mr. Regents and Mr. Scholars Club for the Scholars Club at Langston University respectively. He also works as a mentor and tutor with Cameron University's Open Doors Program. Maurice is active in the community and his local church, teaching youth and young adults.

Maurice is often heard saying, "Everyone wants to be successful and reach their dreams. I live to help others be successful and reach their dreams and live their best life."

To contact Maurice R. Dowell for speaking engagements or coaching, he can be reached on his social media platforms or through his email.

-email @mauricedowell@yahoo.com

-Instagram & Twitter @ Mauricerdowell

-Snapchat, TikTok & Facebook @Mauricedowell

Made in the USA
Las Vegas, NV
29 November 2020